CUTTING EDGE MEDICINE

Machines in Medicine

Anne Rooney

WORLD ALMANAC® LIBRARY

Please visit our Web site at: **www.garethstevens.com**
For a free color catalog describing World Almanac® Library's list of high-quality books
and multimedia programs, call 1-800-848-2928 (USA) or 1-800-387-3178 (Canada).
World Almanac® Library's fax: (414) 332-3567.

Library of Congress Cataloging-in-Publication Data available upon request from publisher.
Fax (414) 336-0157 for the attention of the Publishing Records Department.

Rooney, Anne.
    Machines in medicine / Anne Rooney.
        p. cm. — (Cutting edge medicine)
    Includes bibliographical references and index.
    ISBN 978-0-8368-7867-7 (lib. bdg.)
    1. Medical instruments and apparatus—Juvenile literature.   2. Medical instruments and apparatus—
Juvenile literature.   3. Medical technology—Juvenile literature.   I. Title.
    R856.2.R66   2006
    610.28—dc22   2006030897

This North American edition first published in 2007 by
World Almanac® Library
A Member of the WRC Media Family of Companies
330 West Olive Street, Suite 100
Milwaukee, WI 53212 USA

Produced by Arcturus Publishing Limited.
Editor: Alex Woolf
Designer: Nick Phipps
Consultant: Dr. Eleanor Clarke

World Almanac® Library editor: Carol Ryback
World Almanac® Library designer: Kami M. Strunsee
World Almanac® Library art direction: Tammy West
World Almanac® Library production: Jessica Yanke and Robert Kraus

The right of Andrew Solway to be identified as the author of this work has been
asserted by him in accordance with the Copyright, Designs and Patents Act, 1988.

Photo credits: Science Photo Library: / CC Studio 4; / Sheila Terry 7; / Geoff Tompkinson 8; / Damien Lovegrove 10;
/ Tracy Dominey 12; / Steve Allen 14; / Jim Varney 16; / Maximilianstock Ltd. 19; / Gusto 20; / Samuel Ashfield 23;
/ Malcolm Fielding, the BOC Group plc. 25; / AJ Photo 27; / Stanley B. Burns, M.D., and the Burns Archive, N.Y. 28;
/ Eye of Science 30; / Pascal Goetgheluck 32; / Peter Menzel 34; / Deep Light Productions 36; / Du Cane Medical Imaging
Ltd. 39; / Antonia Reeve 40; / Hank Morgan 43; / BSIP/Laurent/H. Americain 44; / SIU 46; / Sovereign, ISM 49;
/ James King-Holmes 51; / Volker Steger, Peter Arnold Inc. 52; / Hattie Young 55; / Mauro Fermariello 56;
/ Christian Darkin 58).

Printed in China

1 2 3 4 5 6 7 8 9 10 10 09 08 07 06

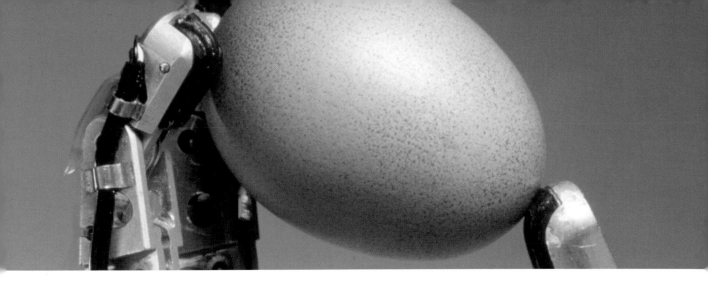

Contents

CHAPTER 1

What's the Problem?

Someone who gets sick in the twenty-first century stands a much better chance of survival and full recovery than a person who got sick one hundred or even fifty years ago. Improved understanding of the human body and how it works has enabled doctors to diagnose and treat illness more effectively. Along with this knowledge, many tools, instruments, and medical equipment have been developed and refined that help medical staff treat patients at all stages of care. Tools range from simple items, such as thermometers, to very sophisticated machinery controlled by computers, to tiny instruments manipulated under a microscope.

Although simple, the stethoscope is an invaluable tool for listening to body sounds.

As increasingly complicated equipment becomes available, medical staff can identify and treat problems more quickly and in different ways. Many people owe their lives to machines used in medicine, and many more depend on them to live normal lives.

A doctor's expertise

Doctors train for many years and are experts at diagnosis (figuring out why someone is sick). An important part of diagnosis is talking to patients, asking them how they feel, and getting the patients to describe how their problem developed. Not all patients can talk to a doctor, however. Babies and young children, or people who are unconscious or in severe pain or distress, cannot answer questions. In such cases, the doctor must examine the patient and look for symptoms (signs of illness or injury). Medical tools and equipment can reveal symptoms that the doctor may not notice and that even the patient cannot identify.

Simple machines

A doctor will often check a patient's temperature, listen to his or her heart and lungs, and perhaps look into the patient's eyes, ears, and mouth. These simple tests use equipment that has been around for centuries—but sometimes, with the expertise of a doctor or health care worker, they are enough to reveal what is wrong.

CUTTING EDGE MOMENTS

Important early medical inventions

Who	What
René-Théophile-Hyacinthe Laënnec (1781–1826)	Invented the first stethoscope in 1816. It was a wooden cylinder 12 inches (30 centimeters) long.
Hermann von Helmholtz (1821–1894)	Invented the ophthalmoscope in 1850, allowing doctors to see the living retina for the first time.
John Brunton (1836–1899)	Invented the otoscope for looking inside ears in 1862.
Sir Thomas Clifford Allbutt (1836–1925)	Invented the clinical thermometer in 1866, allowing a patient's temperature to be measured in a few minutes. Previously it had taken more than 20 minutes to measure temperatures with an instrument 12 inches (30 cm) long.
Samuel Siegfried Karl Ritter von Basch (1837–1905)	Invented the first sphygmomanometer in 1881. It consisted of a water-filled bag connected to a manometer (pressure meter).
Scipione Riva-Rocci (1863–1937)	Developed the mercury sphygmomanometer—the basis of the modern device—in 1896.

Thermometer A classical thermometer, used to measure body temperature, is a glass tube with a column of expanding liquid inside and a scale marked up the side—although most doctors now use a digital thermometer. Thermometers help diagnose an unusually high or low temperature. High temperature is an indication of fever—a symptom of many illnesses.

Otoscope An otoscope is used to look inside the ear. It has a light and a magnifying lens in the tip, which is put just inside the outer ear. The doctor looks through the lens to see the inside of the ear canal and eardrum. A doctor uses an otoscope to see if the ear is infected, damaged, or blocked.

Sphygmomanometer A sphygmomanometer measures blood pressure. A rubber cuff is fitted tightly around the arm while a doctor or nurse pumps air into it, then listens to a patient's pulse with a stethoscope and reads the blood pressure from a dial. A sphygmomanometer is used to detect unusually high or low blood pressure. High blood pressure is common in people with blocked blood vessels or with heart conditions.

Stethoscope A stethoscope magnifies sounds from the heart, lungs, and other organs. It has a "cup" at one end with a flexible flap and tubes that lead to earpieces. The doctor, nurse, or technologist places the cup of the stethoscope over the body area of interest. The stethoscope can help diagnose abnormal heart sounds, irregular lung function, and a variety of abdominal sounds.

CUTTING EDGE SCIENCE

Ultrasound stethoscopes

Ultrasound is produced by a crystal, similar to that in a quartz watch, vibrating about two million times a second. The high-frequency sound waves travel through liquid but are reflected back from solid objects, which produces an echo that is detected by the stethoscope. It can measure the sounds reflected back as blood cells move through the vessels, even under layers of fat in an obese patient. It can also detect the heartbeat of an unborn child inside its mother.

A doctor measures
a patient's blood pressure
using a stethoscope and
a sphygmomanometer.

Ophthalmoscope An ophthalmoscope has a light and a magnifying lens for looking into the eye. The light bounces off the back of the eye (the retina), illuminating it for the doctor or ophthalmologist (an eye specialist). The opthalmoscope reveals problems inside the eyeball, such as problems with the blood vessels lining the eye. An eyeball is directly linked to the brain, so the ophthalmoscope may also reveal other problems with blood vessels not local to the eye.

Getting better all the time

Even the simplest of tools have been greatly improved by modern technology, increasing precision and reducing the possibility of human error.

Since the 1990s, accurate and sensitive digital thermometers have been in common use. They give a precise reading of body temperature within seconds.

Newer otoscopes combine fiber-optic light and a digital screen and produce a range of tones to help test hearing.

Digital sphygmomanometers show a read-out of blood pressure on a screen, indicate if the cuff is not properly placed on the arm, and automatically inflate and deflate the cuff.

Sophisticated stethoscopes that work with ultrasound (high-pitched sounds) can measure the flow of blood in blood vessels deep inside the body and can help assess heart conditions. Ultrasound stethoscopes reveal narrowed or blocked vessels that hinder blood flow and lead to serious problems, such as stroke.

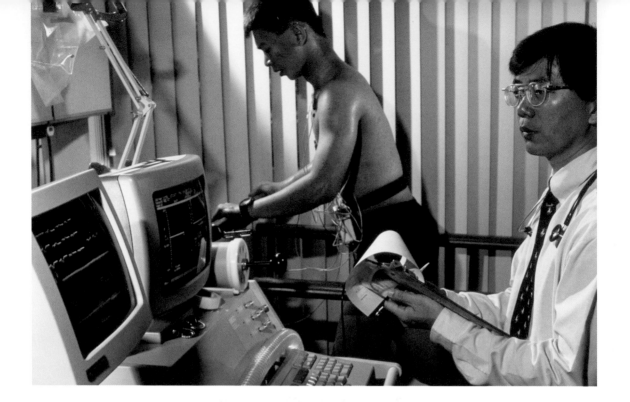

An electrocardiograph machine monitors a patient's heartbeat through electrodes attached to his chest as he exercises.

Electric bodies

The human body creates tiny pulses of electricity that carry messages around the nervous system, the network of nerves and nerve cells that enables us to sense the outside world and to control our muscles. Instruments that detect these electrical pulses monitor conditions in the body and diagnose problems.

Electrocardiograph An electrocardiograph (EKG) measures the electric pulses in the muscles of the heart. Electrodes (pads or wires that pick up electric current) fastened to the patient's body, usually on the chest and hands, detect electric current from the heart. The EKG produces a graph called an electrocardiogram. If a patient has a healthy heart, the graph shows regular peaks as the muscles of the heart expand and contract. An irregular heartbeat, abnormally sized chambers of the heart, and some blood pressure problems can be diagnosed from an unusual pattern on an electrocardiogram.

Electroencephalograph An electroencephalograph (EEG) measures brain activity using pairs of electrodes placed on the scalp. The brain is packed with nerve cells and produces lots of electrical activity. An EEG, which produces a graph similar to an EKG, helps diagnose brain tumors, epilepsy, injuries, infections of the brain, and some diseases that affect the nerves.

Electromyelograph An electromyelograph (EMG) measures electrical pulses in the muscles. It is used to check muscle activity and the action of the nerves controlling the muscles. AN EMG can help diagnose the causes of muscle weakness by revealing whether it is caused by disorders of the nerves, such as carpal tunnel syndrome, or deterioration of the muscles themselves, such as muscular dystrophy. A thin electrode, like a hypodermic needle, is pushed into the muscle and attached to an oscilloscope, a device for measuring electric current. When the patient uses the muscle—bending an arm or leg, for instance—a current is measured and produces a similar graph to an EKG or an EEG.

Portable tests

Small, portable EEG and EKG equipment allows doctors and paramedics to diagnose some problems at the scene of an emergency. This is particularly useful for diagnosing heart attacks and stroke, which require immediate treatment. Some portable machines can transmit data directly from the equipment to a distant receiver.

CUTTING EDGE MOMENTS

Measuring the body's electricity

1884	John Burden Sanderson and Frederick Page (England) record the heart's electrical current, showing it has two phases.
1887	Augustus Waller (England) makes the first electrocardiogram.
1895	Willem Einthoven (the Netherlands) identifies five different phases of electrical current shown in a electrocardiogram.
1905	Willem Einthoven transmits electrocardiograms 1 mile (1.5 kilometers) from the hospital to his lab via telephone cables.
1924	Hans Berger (Germany) recorded the first electroencephalogram.
1928	Frank Sanborn's company (United States) produces the first portable EKG.
2005	In Denmark, data from an EKG in an ambulance is transmitted by wireless network to the Personal Digital Assistant (PDA) of a cardiologist at a hospital, who makes a remote diagnosis.

Breathing

Medical machinery can help diagnose and treat lung problems for people with breathing disorders, such as asthma. One of the first tasks in diagnosing breathing difficulties is to measure the lung capacity, often using a device called a peak flow meter. A peak flow

A peak flow meter is a simple way of measuring lung function. Many patients use them at home to monitor the condition of their lungs.

meter consists of a plastic tube and a slider that moves along a numbered scale showing the volume of air exhaled (breathed out). It measures the amount of air a person can breathe in and blow out. This amount is called the forced vital capacity of the lungs. If the volume of air is less than 80 percent of the average for a person of that size and age, the patient may need treatment to improve his or her lung function.

The digital spirometer is a more sophisticated tool for measuring lung function. It also measures the forced vital capacity of a patient's lungs, but the technology is more refined and accurate. The volume and force of the patient's exhalation is measured by an electronic sensor and is compared with other data stored in the spirometer (or on a computer) to compare the reading with expected or average levels or to track the patient's progress. Using a digital spirometer, a doctor can determine the patient's lung capacity, the rate at which air flows through the lungs, as well as the tidal volume—the amount of air breathed in and out when the patient breathes normally. The measurements can reveal obstructions or restrictions in the lungs and airways.

CUTTING EDGE   SCIENTISTS

Basil Martin Wright

Bioengineer Basil Wright (1912–2001) had a flare for invention. In 1949, he joined the Medical Research Council's unit for pneumoconiosis (a lung disease caused by inhaling mineral or metallic dust). He found that the unit, based at Llandough, Wales, lacked the equipment needed to undertake large-scale studies of lung capacity. To remedy the situation, he invented the first peak flow meter in 1959. This made studies of lung function possible and led to a greater understanding of lung disease. The first peak flow meters were large and cumbersome, but Wright designed a personal, portable model in 1974. Many people with asthma use these at home to monitor their lung function. Wright moved to the National Institute for Medical Research in London, England, in 1957 and concentrated solely on developing new instruments. He invented a device called a respirometer, which is still used to give anesthetics (pain-relieving drugs) to patients during surgery and to administer continuous pain relief to dying patients. The roadside breathalyzer used by the police to test drivers' breath for alcohol is based on Wright's respirometer.

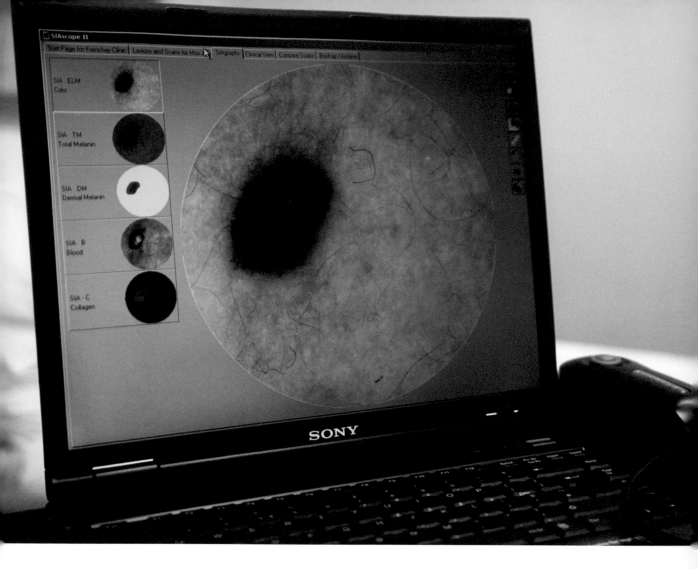

The following text labels appear on the computer screen in the image:

SIAscope II

Start Page for Frenchay Clinic | Lesions and Scans for Miss | SIAgraphs | Clinical View | Compare Scans | Backup / Archive

SIA ELM
Color

SIA TM
Total Melanin

SIA DM
Dermal Melanin

SIA B
Blood

SIA - C
Collagen

SONY

Computers in diagnosis

Until fairly recently, doctors had to depend on reference charts, books, and their own knowledge to diagnose and treat a patient's condition. While these are still invaluable—the expertise and intuition of doctors can never be replaced by technology—computers are taking on an increasingly important role.

A medical expert system is a computer program that brings together the knowledge of many experts. It provides a comprehensive resource that can be shared by doctors everywhere to take some of the guesswork out of diagnosis. Expert systems draw upon extensive records and information about a wide range of diseases and disorders. These computer programs search and analyze all such information within seconds.

By combining the results of all the tests that a doctor or hospital has run on a patient, an expert system can make intelligent

A computer is used with a portable device called a SIAscope. It aids in the diagnosis of skin lesions, such as this mole, shown in a magnified view on the screen.

diagnoses or suggestions. This saves time because the comparison and analysis is practically instantaneous. The program also draws on more expertise than a single doctor or specialist is ever likely to know. Expert systems are especially good for spotting unusual conditions that a doctor may not think of or even have come across before. A human doctor usually fares better than a computer if the patient's symptoms are the result of two or more conditions, however. While the computer first looks for a condition that combines all the symptoms, a doctor may recognize groups of symptoms that lead him or her to suspect there is more than one condition affecting the patient.

In hospitals, computers can be used with various types of scanners to produce three-dimensional images of the inside of the body, often vital in spotting problems and directing surgery. After human experts have confirmed a diagnosis, the computer can help again by presenting possibilities for treatment and modeling outcomes and risks for different treatments.

Asking questions

Patients can even diagnose their own conditions in some cases by using an online computer database. The patient fills in a questionnaire on a screen, and the computer will attempt to diagnose the problem. Sometimes, patients may be able to avoid a doctor or hospital visit completely if they can diagnose a simple condition that is not immediately dangerous to their health.

CUTTING EDGE   SCIENCE

Fuzzy logic and diagnostics

Expert systems use a technique called "fuzzy logic." This works on approximations and probabilities rather than absolute numbers. Instead of trying to match symptoms precisely to illnesses, fuzzy logic assesses how well symptoms match expected symptoms for different illnesses, while allowing for degrees of variation. This is a more reliable basis for medical diagnosis, because the symptoms are likely to vary by patient. Strict rules for diagnosing a patient's condition could lead to a large number of misdiagnoses since the fuzzy logic might exclude possible disorders too readily.

CHAPTER 2

In the Laboratory

A visit to a doctor or clinic is often just the first stage of diagnosis. Technologists may perform much work behind the scenes examining and analyzing samples taken from the patient, such as blood and fluid, biopsies (small pieces of tissue removed either by surgery or with a needle), or cell scrapings. The tests look for abnormal patterns of growth, abnormally shaped cells, and viruses and bacteria (microorganisms that can cause disease).

Microscopes

Microscopes provide a magnified view of items too small to see with the naked eye. Simple

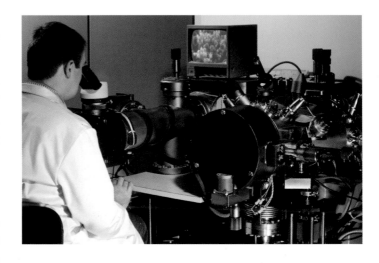

A researcher uses a scanning electron microscope to examine blood cells.

microscopes use only one lens, while compound microscopes use several. Some microscopes have a single eyepiece; most, called binocular microscopes, have two eyepieces so that the user can view the object with both eyes. Certain microscopes are connected to computers and can project the magnified image onto a screen, make measurements, and make comparisons and calculations. For example, a doctor can use a microscope to compare healthy cells and diseased cells that may be cancerous. A cell from the human body may be only 10 microns across. (1 micron is 1/25,000 of an inch or 0.001 of a millimeter.) A microscope connected to a computer can store images from different samples and bring them up for a side-by-side comparison.

Preparing samples

Microscopes are used to look at fluid or solid body samples. Either may be dyed with a number of different chemical stains that reveal particular structures or materials in distinct colors. For example, bacteria that are causing an infection may be revealed in a stained smear sample. Samples are usually placed on a slide (a thin plate of glass), stained, and covered with a glass cover.

Oftentimes, biological samples are treated with a chemical called a fixative, which stops changes from taking place in the sample. The fixative usually preserves the fluid or tissue in as close to a lifelike state as possible. Samples that are not "fixed" and that contain enzymes or microorganisms, can begin to decompose, or deteriorate, making the sample less useful. The cellular breakdown may affect the shape, staining, or appearance of the sample and cause a misdiagnosis.

After fixation, solid body tissues are described and measured, cut into a smaller representative piece, and then dehydrated. Each piece is set in paraffin wax and sliced very thin on a special machine. A see-through tissue section is placed on a glass slide, stained, and coverslipped. A doctor called a pathologist will examine the tissue slide under a microsope and make a diagnosis from what is seen.

CUTTING EDGE   SCIENCE

Microscopes

Modern microscopes range from small optical (light) microscopes to large and powerful scanning and transmission electron microscopes. An optical microscope uses lenses to magnify the image by bending rays of light. The level of magnification for optical microscopes is limited by the wavelength of light, which eventually causes the image to distort.

An electron microscope uses magnetic lenses to focus beams of electrons (very tiny components of the atoms that make up all matter). The wavelength of a beam of electrons is much smaller than that of light, and accurate, clear images can be achieved at greater magnifications. There are two types of electron microscope. A scanning electron microscope (SEM) is used for looking at the surface of objects. A transmission electron microscope (TEM) fires electrons straight through a sample. It produces a high-resolution image (showing much detail) and can give information about the internal structure of the sample.

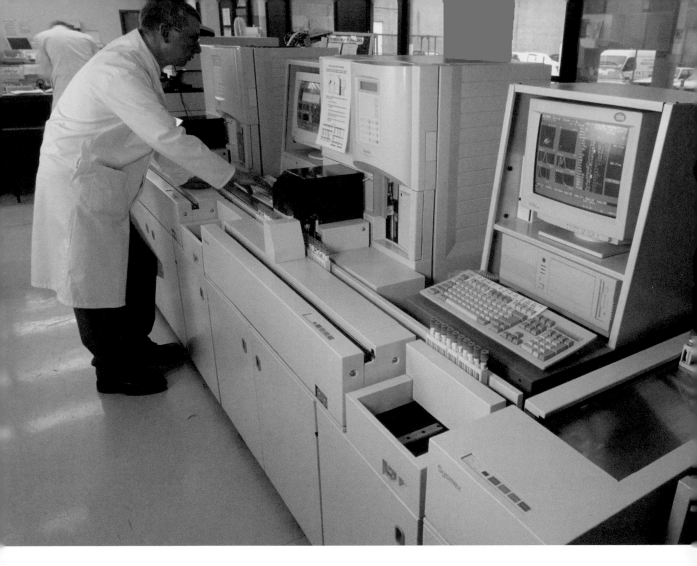

A technician analyzes
blood using a machine
called a Coulter counter.

Picking out problems

After receiving a sample from a patient, laboratory staff select the areas they want to look at, either isolating them from the sample or identifying them under the microscope. Sometimes, solids are extracted from a liquid sample by centrifuging (spinning at high speed) or filtering the liquid.

Researchers can stain or dye a sample to show the cellular features that they need to see. The dye stains different cell structures differently, and the amount of dye that is absorbed indicates the densities or compositions of material in the sample. Dyes can reveal harmful microorganisms such as bacteria, and abnormalities in or damage to body tissue or cells.

Some bacteria, known as gram-positive because they absorb a purple dye called gram, look purple or blue. Others don't retain the dye well and look pink. These are gram-negative bacteria. Using the

A technician analyzes blood using a machine called a Coulter counter.

gram dye can help narrow the possibilities when diagnosing a bacterial infection.

Sometimes, a special type of dye is injected into tissue before a sample is taken. Radioactive dyes—dyes that emit a small amount of radioactivity (beams of energy)—may be injected near a cancerous growth, for example. A surgeon can then detect the radioactive areas and take a biopsy sample from them. By using dyes known to bind to particular cancer cells, the surgeon can ensure that exactly the right cells are removed for examination.

Counters and analyzers

Many samples are taken with the goal of counting or identifying cells or features of a certain type. In a blood sample, for instance, the investigation may include a blood count, a count of all the cells present in the blood—and in what quantities. For example, allergies and the disease leukemia lead to unusually high numbers of certain types of white blood cells; too few red blood cells is a symptom of a condition called anemia. During fertility treatments, a man may be asked to provide a semen sample for a sperm count. If there are fewer than the normal number of sperm, the man may be experiencing low fertility. Sperm counts are carried out automatically by a computerized device called a semen analyzer.

CUTTING EDGE   SCIENCE

Laser tweezers
Sometimes it is necessary to separate different types of cells, such as healthy cells from diseased cells. Individual cells and parts of cells can be picked out or moved around using laser or optical tweezers. These use beams of light to move cells or parts of cells without damaging them. Laser beams are spread into intricate patterns or moved rapidly by a system of moving mirrors. A pattern of interconnecting laser beams acts like a trap or a mesh of light, letting through only particles smaller than the mesh. Moving laser beams can also nudge particles into position. This technique can be used to move tiny strands of DNA into a cell during research into or treatment of inherited diseases. The most advanced laser tweezers can also be used for spectroscopy—measuring how the particles scatter laser light reveals their shape, sizes, and chemical composition.

Profilers

Complex systems incorporating several machines can provide a complete profile of a sample when multiple tests are needed. These make various measurements and analyses and combines the results to give an accurate result. For example, profiling a blood sample will give a complete blood count and also provide information about the levels of chemicals, hormones (natural "messenger" chemicals released into the bloodstream), nutrients, and any contaminants (chemicals that should not be present) in the blood.

DNA profiling is a method of finding out about a patient's genetic makeup. DNA is the material from which genes and chromosomes are made. Every person has a unique genetic makeup, and a complete DNA profile, or genome, is like a genetic map. A DNA profile can be used to match a sample with an individual, for example, by identifying the victim of an accident. Or it can be used to pinpoint specific features, such as identifying a hereditary disease or disorder. DNA profiling can be used to test embryos (the early stages of the developing fertilized egg before it implants in the uterine wall and becomes a fetus) produced during in vitro fertilization (the procedure that unites egg and sperm in the laboratory) to exclude any with an inherited disorder. Any embryos found to have an inherited disorder will be rejected and not implanted.

CUTTING EDGE — SCIENCE

Spotting cells

Samples of body fluids (other than blood) are usually examined under a microscope by a cytologist—a cell expert. This is a time-consuming process, prone to human error. Computer image-matching systems are replacing some human screening of pap smear slides produced to detect cervical cancer in women. The computer takes images from a camera and microscope and compares them with images of the nuclei of normal and cancerous cells. If a cell appears to match a cancerous type, the computer flags it, and the cells are more carefully analyzed.

Chemical tests

Other complex chemical procedures are often used with liquid samples such as blood, urine, and other body fluids.

Mass spectrometry measures the mass of molecules and determines the chemical composition of a sample. In blood samples, it can detect performance-enhancing drugs taken by athletes.

A scientist examines a test tube of liquid separated from a sample using chromatography.

Chromatography is a method of separating and identifying the components of a liquid or gas. The sample is mixed with a carrier, either as a liquid or gas, and moves over a stationary bed of an absorbent material.

Different components are absorbed at different rates or travel further through the column of absorbent material. Technicians read the results as a line graph consisting of a series of peaks. The position of the peaks and the area under them indicate the concentrations of different components.

Gel electrophoresis uses an electrical charge to separate molecules (tiny particles that are the smallest component of a substance) of different sizes in a sample set in gel. Charged particles move toward or away from a source of electricity. The speed of their movement reveals their sizes (the largest molecules move the slowest). Technicians read the results as a series of shaded strips. The amount of shading indicates the percentages of the different components.

CHAPTER 3

Emergency!

Not all medical investigations occur in an orderly fashion. Often, medical staff must deal with emergency situations, such as accidents, where every second counts. The patient's survival or full recovery may depend on the care he or she receives in the first few critical minutes, and medical machinery can be a lifesaver.

Breathing problems

Sudden breathing difficulties can be very dangerous. The brain needs oxygen all the time to function, and if disturbances to breathing limit the amount of oxygen carried in the blood, brain damage and death occur quickly. People may suffer breathing difficulties for many reasons, but one of the most common is a

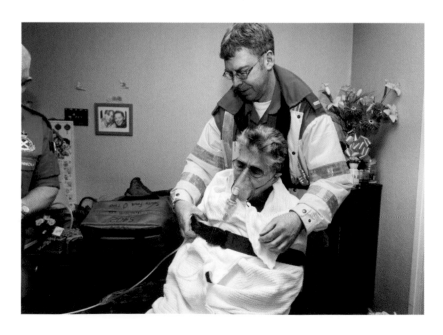

A paramedic assists an elderly patient suffering from breathing difficulties. Prompt action is vital in emergencies involving lung function.

sudden asthma attack. This is often treated using a machine called a nebulizer, which produces a very fine aerosol (spray) of medicine suspended as tiny droplets in the air. The nebulizer delivers the medicine through the patient's nose and mouth to the lungs, where it relaxes the muscles and opens the constricted airways.

A number of situations cause patients to need extra oxygen quickly. Oxygen is usually supplied from an external tank through a mask that covers the patient's nose and mouth. If extra oxygen is needed to help recover from more serious breathing problems, the patient is sometimes placed in a chamber that delivers oxygen under high pressure for hyperbaric oxygen therapy.

The high oxygen pressure in the hyperbaric chamber increases the rate at which the blood can absorb oxygen and transport it to tissues that need it. A compression chamber can help scuba divers with decompression sickness (caused by surfacing from a dive too quickly) and is used to treat stubborn wounds that will not heal, to treat types of radiation sickness, and to treat carbon monoxide poisoning (common in people rescued from house fires). The high-pressure chamber delivers the oxygen to the patient more efficiently than can a small oxygen tank on wheels because the chamber exerts extra pressure on the outside of the body.

CUTTING EDGE   SCIENCE

Hyperbaric oxygen therapy (HBOT)

Hyperbaric oxygen therapy involves giving patients oxygen at more than normal atmospheric pressure. Patients are commonly treated in a large metal chamber that can hold several people at once. Each patient wears a transparent plastic hood that delivers the oxygen. They are attended by a specially trained doctor, nurse, or technologist. Patients can stand, sit, or lie down and may be able to watch videos, read, or sleep while receiving the treatment.

New capillaries (very tiny blood vessels) form quickly in wounded areas as a response to the extra oxygen. When breathed in under pressure, the oxygen travels two to three times farther into the tissue capillaries. The increased circulation aids healing. The super-oxygenated blood also doubles or triples the ability of the white blood cells to destroy some harmful bacteria.

Heart and blood

Among the most common emergencies involving the heart and the circulatory system (the system of blood vessels) are heart attack and stroke. In a heart attack, an artery (a blood vessel carrying oxygenated blood) in the heart becomes blocked, and part of the heart muscle stops functioning. Within three to four minutes of a heart attack, the heart stops beating and must be restarted very quickly if the patient is to survive. In a stroke, the blood supply to the brain is interrupted, usually because a blood clot (a lump of solidifying blood) is blocking an artery.

A paramedic with a portable EKG (*see pages 8 and 9*) can confirm the diagnosis of heart attack, measure the functioning of the heart, and determine the severity of the damage caused by the heart attack. If the heart stops beating properly, it can be restarted with a defibrillator. This uses pads containing electrodes that, when attached to the patient's chest, pass an electric shock to the heart to jolt it into beating regularly.

The early defibrillators were about the size and weight of a car battery and not easy to transport. The first portable model was designed by physician and cardiologist Frank Pantridge, from County Down, Northern Ireland. He also developed the idea of providing coronary care in ambulances. Many ambulances now carry defibrillators. Planes and some public buildings also have

CUTTING EDGE SCIENTISTS

Mieczyslaw Mirowski

Mieczyslaw Mirowski (1924–1990) was born in Warsaw, Poland. At different periods of his life, he lived in Poland, Israel, France (where he trained in medicine), Mexico, and the United States. In 1966, while in Israel, the death of a close colleague from heart disease inspired him to develop a ventricular defibrillator that could be implanted directly into the heart. It would restart a person's heart that had stopped. The medical profession did not support Mirowski's plan, which was considered unworkable. He fought professional opposition and lack of funding before successfully completing a prototype in 1975. After testing on dogs, the first AID (automatic implantable defibrillator) was implanted in a human patient in 1980. Over the next five years, eight hundred patients received an AID.

portable defibrillators so that heart attack patients can be treated immediately, thus avoiding a delay that could prove fatal.

A portable defibrillator on an airplane is used to treat a patient who has suffered a cardiac arrest during a flight.

Bleeding

A person who loses a lot of blood can die very quickly. The best way to prevent blood loss after a serious injury is to clamp the severed blood vessel with direct pressure or by using a simple tool called a hemostatic clamp, or hemostat. This instrument looks like a pair of scissors, but with a locking clamp in place of blades.

Since the late 1980s, a substance called microfibrillar collagen hemostat is often applied to wounds in place of mechanical clamps. This substance contains artificial collagen; collagen is the protein that forms the connective tissue that supports and binds together other tissues, such as muscle, blood vessels, and skin. The hemostat attracts platelets (a blood component), which clump together and form a natural clot to stop the bleeding.

Intensive care

When a person is very ill or badly injured, they may need several different kinds of care to treat more than one body system at the same time. Modern hospitals are equipped with intensive care units (ICUs) that have a range of complex machinery that monitors body functions and helps provide constant and immediate care. These machines can keep alive a patient who would die without this level of care—for example, people suffering from extreme breathing problems, kidney failure, multi-organ failure, or sepsis (blood poisoning).

The first intensive care unit was established in Copenhagen, Denmark, in 1953 by Dr. Bjorn Ibsen in response to a polio epidemic, which left many victims with severe breathing difficulties that required artificial ventilation.

Patients in an ICU are connected to monitors that track vital signs, such as heart rate, blood pressure, temperature, breathing rate, and the levels of oxygen and carbon dioxide in their blood.

CUTTING EDGE   DEBATES

Turning off the machine

Patients can often be kept alive on a life support system in an ICU long beyond the point when they would have died without such advanced care. Some patients can be sustained indefinitely, though they have no chance of recovering and living a normal life. If a patient has no chance of recovery, medical staff may suggest that the artificial ventilators be turned off, or that feeding through tubes is withdrawn, and the patient is allowed to die. It is a contentious issue, and when there are disagreements between medical staff and family members, the courts may be called on to decide whether the patient should remain on life support or be disconneted and allowed to die.

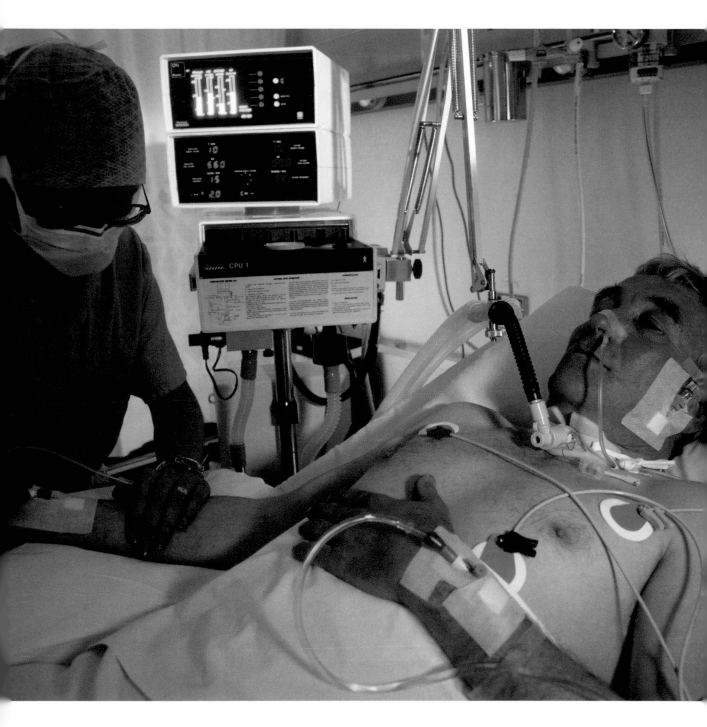

Computers combine the data from the different monitors to provide a real-time, complete report of the patient's vital signs at a glance. Display screens and warning systems in the ICU immediately alert the medical staff to any changes in the patient's condition.

A patient in the ICU is constantly monitored and receives treatments from an array of medical machinery.

Some people in intensive care need help with breathing or with the function of organs such as the kidneys. A ventilator takes over the task of breathing for the patient. A ventilator is a machine that pumps the right amount of air into the lungs at the right pressure, mimicking the person's normal breathing.

Neonatal care

Very tiny infants need specialized care and specially adapted medical equipment. Newborn and premature infants (those born before they have spent nine months in the uterus) have delicate and finely balanced systems. The lungs of premature infants are often underdeveloped, and they will likely need assistance with breathing while they continue to grow.

Very ill newborns and "preemies" (premature infants) are cared for in a special neonatal intensive care unit. In the unit, all babies lie in incubators. The incubators provide a temperature-controlled environment that keeps the infant warm. Respiratory distress syndrome, which causes difficulty in breathing, is particularly common in premature infants. These babies need ventilators to help them breathe. Many infants in neonatal intensive care are fed through tubes that go through the nose and down the throat into the stomach; they are too young to efficiently suck milk from a bottle or breast.

CUTTING EDGE   FACTS

Oxygen and infant blindness

The development of incubators that could provide an oxygen-rich environment for infants brought an unexpected problem in the form of retrolental fibroplasias (RLF), a disease that causes blindness by narrowing the arteries in the retina. Doctors noticed the high incidence of RLF in preemies in the 1940s caused by exposure to high concentrations of oxygen in incubators. Withholding the oxygen, however, could cause brain damage or death. In the 1950s, doctors solved the problem by restricting infants' exposure to high levels of oxygen. All babies are now very carefully monitored to make sure they are not suffering damage as a result of too much or too little oxygen, and the incidence of RLF is greatly reduced.

Neonatal intensive care is a specialized branch of medicine requiring expensive high-tech equipment. Some larger hospitals handle all such patients in a wide geographic area. Specially equipped neonatal ambulances transport sick infants to or between neonatal care units. The neonatal ambulances carry incubators and ventilators, so the infant receives continuous care.

Doctors and nurses constantly monitor the vital signs of a premature infant in an incubator in a neonatal unit.

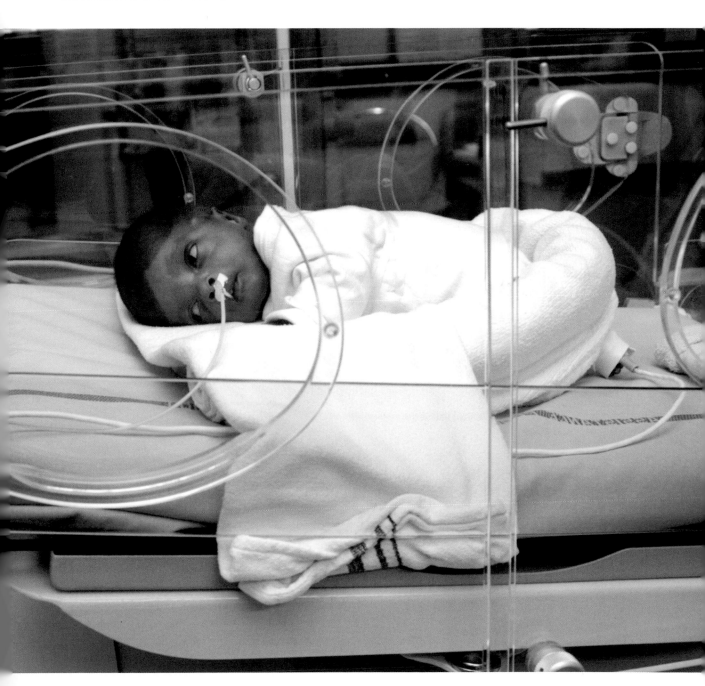

CHAPTER 4

Surgery and Operations

The simplest surgical tools, such as knives and forceps, have been in use for thousands of years. In the ninth century, Arab surgeons developed instruments that are similar to many still in use today. Modern surgeons, however, also draw on an array of machines to help them in their work. Some machines help keep patients stable and anesthetized (unconscious and free of pain) during operations, while other machines assist the surgeon in the operation or surgical procedure itself.

Controlling pain

An anesthetic prevents a patient from feeling pain. In the days before anesthetics were available, surgery could be brutal and

The advent of anesthesia finally made operations like this leg amputation in 1857 bearable for the patient and easier for the surgeon.

Delivering anesthetic gases

An anesthesia machine mixes a vaporized anesthetic with a supply of gases, usually nitrogen and oxygen, and delivers the mix to the patient through a mask or tube. The nitrogen and oxygen are generally piped through the hospital. Supply tubes from the wall are plugged into the machine, which has backup cylinders of gas in case the central supply fails. The machine has one or more vaporizers, which feed measured, small quantities of anesthetic vapor into the flow of gases delivered to the patient. Flow meters and pressure gauges are used to monitor and control the flow so that the patient is not exposed to high pressures. Anesthetic gas is removed from the air breathed out by the patient and discharged outside the room. Monitors, alarms, and safety systems make sure the patient cannot receive too much or too little of any of the components and alert staff if the equipment fails in any way. A patient's vital signs, such as heart rate and breathing rates, are monitored with electronic sensors at all times.

painful for the patient. Patients were often held down by assistants and were sometimes given something, such as a stick, to bite on. The surgeon's work was limited by how long the patient could remain still and endure the pain of surgery. Great progress has been made in surgery since anesthetics have become available.

General anesthetics render patients unconscious: They are unaware of anything happening to them and feel no pain. A local anesthetic works on just one area of the body, making it numb. Whenever possible, surgeons prefer to use a local anesthetic. It causes less stress and disruption to the body and allows the patient to remain communicative. Many local anesthetics are given in the form of an injection of a natural or artificial alkaloid (a type of nitrogen-containing chemical found in plants) such as Novocaine, that numbs the area to be treated.

Block anesthetics are injected near a major nerve to deaden a large area. The best known is the spinal block or epidural anesthetic often given to women during childbirth. This prevents pain messages from being passed up the spinal cord to the brain, so the patient is not aware of any discomfort. A thin tube is connected to a needle inserted into the spine, and the anesthetic is delivered steadily through the tube. Local anesthetics have no lasting effects and wear off quickly without affecting other parts of the body.

General anesthetics may be given by injection or as a gas, which the patient breathes in using a mask that fits over the face; a tube may be passed down the throat into the lungs after the patient is asleep. A qualified anesthetist uses computerized equipment to

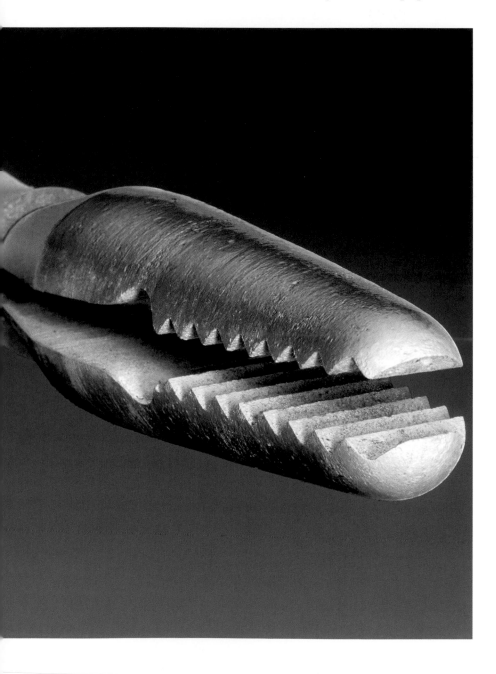

A photograph taken through a microscope of a clamp used in microsurgery on the brain. The clamp is only about 0.02 inch (0.63 mm) in diameter. (That is about the width of the period at the end of this sentence!)

monitor the patient's breathing, heart rate, blood pressure, and the level of oxygen in the blood. If there is any change in these vital signs, the level of anesthetic can be adjusted as necessary. Precise monitoring means that much smaller doses of anesthetic can be used than was previously possible.

Microsurgery

Until recently, surgery was limited by the surgeon's ability to manipulate instruments using the naked eye and his or her own hands. The development of microsurgery has enabled surgeons to carry out far more delicate procedures than was previously possible. In microsurgery, tiny instruments are manipulated with the help of a microscope or magnifying camera and often with the assistance of computers or robots.

Thanks to microsurgery, severed blood vessels can be reattached and nerves can be reconnected, which allows transplanted organs or limbs to function as normally as possible. Operations on the inside of the eye and the inner ear are also possible using microsurgery tools and techniques.

CUTTING EDGE MOMENTS

Landmarks in microsurgery

1921	Carl Olof Nylen (Sweden) first uses a microscope in surgery to perform delicate operations on the ear.
1922	Gunnar Holmgren (Sweden) invents the binocular operating microscope.
1950s	Julius Jacobson and Ernesto Suarez (United States) develop the operating microscope to repair small blood vessels.
1960s	Bernard O'Brien (Australia) pioneers microsurgical techniques, particularly on the attachment and regeneration of bone.
1965	Susumi Tamai (Japan) carries out the first reattachment of a completely severed finger.
1968	John Cobbett (England) transplants a great toe to replace a lost thumb.
1985	First use of robotically controlled tools in microsurgery.
2005	First face transplant carried out in Lyon, France.

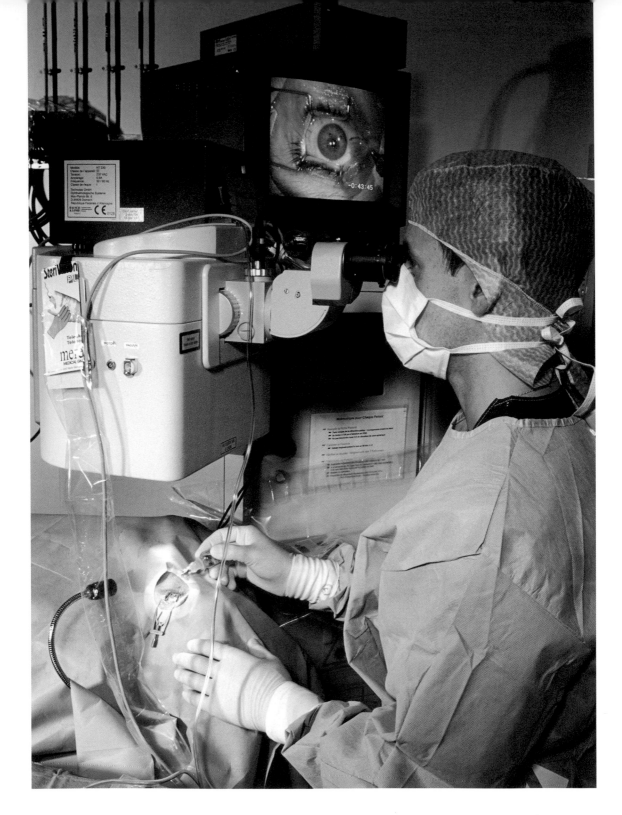

Surgeons operate while looking through a microscope or while using a camera that projects a magnified image of the area being operated on onto a computer screen. The microscopes used for

A surgeon performs laser eye surgery with the help of a microscope connected to a computer.

microsurgery are binocular (they have two eyepieces), which makes it easier for the surgeon to judge distances in three dimensions. Some microscopes have two pairs of eyepieces so that two surgeons can view the operating site at the same time. Surgeons use scaled-down surgical tools to carry out delicate operations.

Procedures that can be performed using microsurgery include the reconnection of severed or torn blood vessels, nerves, tendons, or muscle fibers. During these operations, surgeons often need to make minute sutures (stitches). These are made with nylon or polypropylene only 20 microns thick with a needle that is 50 to 130 microns in diameter. Clamps are available to seal blood vessels with a diameter of less than half a millimeter, and forceps may have tips of only a tenth of a millimeter.

CUTTING EDGE SCIENCE

Laser eye surgery

Lasers are used widely in eye surgery, both for reattaching the retina (the lining of the eye) when it has become detached and to remodel the cornea (the clear membrane over the eye) to correct vision defects. Laser eye surgery, called LASIK, was first performed in 1990 by Lucio Buratto of Italy and Ioannis Pallikaris from Greece.

A map of the patient's cornea is first created using low-power lasers. The patient is given anesthetic eye drops and a sedative, but remains awake for the procedure. The doctor first creates a flap of the top surface of the cornea with a laser and folds it back. He or she then uses a different type of laser to remodel the lower layer, or stroma, of the cornea. The laser vaporizes targeted tissue by destroying the bonds within the molecules. When enough of the stroma has been removed, the outer flap is folded back over the top of the eyeball. The patient's vision is corrected, and the eye heals naturally.

Lasers

Lasers (short for light amplification by simulated emission of radiation) are high-powered, intensely focused, and narrow beams of light that can be precisely targeted. A laser can produce very high temperatures, but cool lasers used in surgery are directed at a very small area and do not heat nearby tissue.

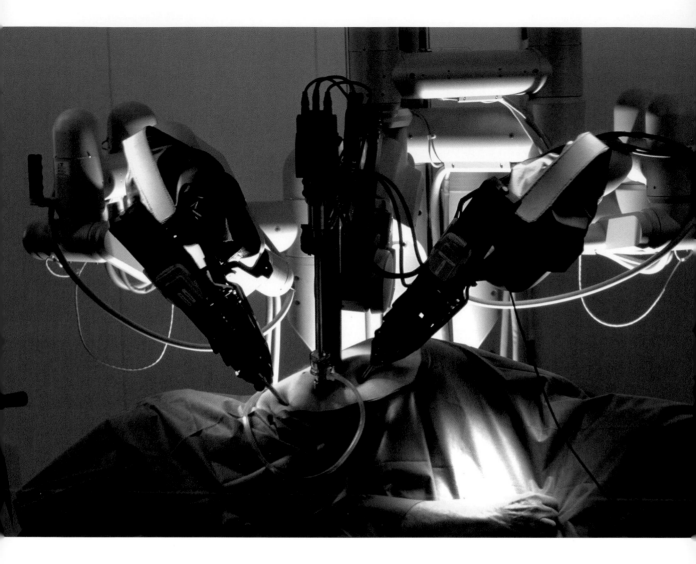

A laser scalpel cuts or—more accurately—burns through tissue without damaging adjoining tissue, which can happen when a conventional scalpel (surgical knife) is used. The laser scalpel automatically cauterizes (seals) the wound it creates, stopping any bleeding by heat-sealing the ends of blood vessels. Lasers can also be used to stop the bleeding caused by a peptic ulcer (damage to the lining of the intestine).

Lasers can be used to cut through bone and to destroy tissue, such as cancerous growths (carcinomas). Lasers can also be used as a replacement for mechanical drills in dentistry.

Colored tissue (for example, a tissue that contains a lot of blood) is particularly sensitive to lasers. The laser can destroy colored

The da Vinci medical robot performs an operation on a patient's heart, working through an incision (cut) only 0.5 inch (1 cm) long. The surgeon observes the operation by watching images captured by a camera on one of the robotic arms. He or she controls the camera and surgical tools remotely.

carcinomas or skin blotches known as Rosacea, and can destroy the pigment in tattoos, removing the tattoo.

Robots in surgery

In physical tasks, robots can often perform better than a human being. They do not get tired, they do not suffer from tremors or slips, they can make very small and precise movements, and they are not limited by the size of the human hand. Robots are increasingly used in surgery to manipulate tiny instruments in very small spaces inside the body. The expertise of the surgeon is still needed to direct the tools: Robotic surgery is an extension of human skills, not a replacement for them.

Robots may be passive or active. A passive robot may align and position equipment, but a human surgeon carries out the surgical procedure itself.

An active robot, however, performs surgical procedures. Active robots are already commonly used in joint replacement surgery and to destroy stones or cancerous growths from within the body.

CUTTING EDGE MOMENTS

Robotics and telesurgery

1985	The first use of a robot, the PUMA 560, to place a needle for a brain biopsy, at Memorial Hospital in Los Angeles, California.
1988	The first human surgery to be carried out by robot, using the "Probot" at Imperial College, London, England, on a patient with prostate cancer.
1992	Integrated Surgical Systems, based in Davis, California, develop the ROBODOC to remove bone ready for a hip replacement operation.
1997	Approval by the U.S. Food and Drug Administration of the da Vinci Surgical System as the first assisting surgical robot. It was manufactured by Intuitive Surgical Inc., based in Sunnyvale, California.
1998	The first robotic surgery is performed at the Broussais Hospital in Paris, France.
2001	The first transatlantic telesurgery: A surgeon in New York City removes the gall bladder of a patient in Strasbourg, France.

Long-distance surgery

The combination of robotically controlled tools and fast computer networks replaces the need for a surgeon to be physically present to perform a surgery. A camera connected to a computer can send a live video feed from the operating room to a surgeon in another location, who instructs helpers and controls robotic tools. The surgeon may use controls that mimic the sensation of actually performing the operation—he or she can "feel" the pressure of a blade pushing against bone, for example.

The remote use of robots for surgery is called telesurgery. It is particularly useful when an emergency situation arises somewhere that a doctor cannot easily access, such as on an oil rig, a ship, or even a spacecraft. A Canadian medical team is experimenting with

A heart-lung machine (in the foreground) is being used to pump and oxygenate a patient's blood during heart bypass surgery.

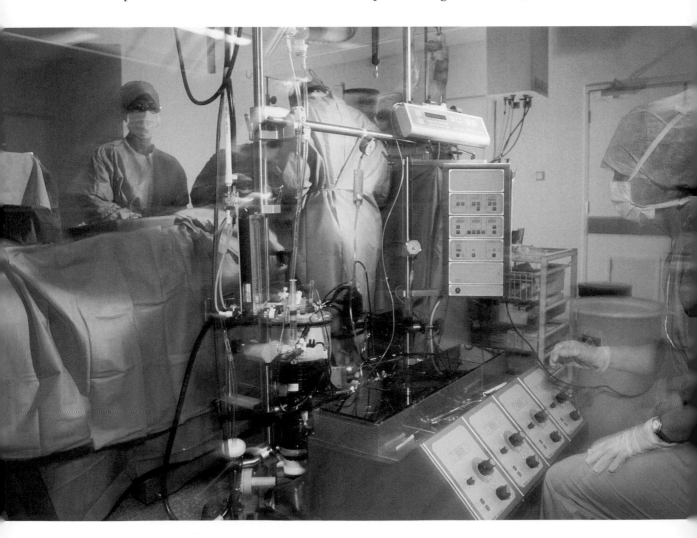

performing telesurgery techniques in a mock spacecraft. They practice in "zero-gravity" conditions underwater. Telesurgery is still in its infancy, but is developing rapidly.

CUTTING EDGE — SCIENTISTS

John Heysham Gibbon

John Gibbon (1903–1973) was born in Philadelphia, Pennsylvania, into a family of doctors. He trained at Princeton University, New Jersey, in 1923 and at Jefferson Medical College in Philadelphia, qualifying as a doctor in 1927. Upset by the death of a young patient in 1931, Gibbon resolved to find a way of bypassing the heart and lungs to make surgery on the heart possible. Despite the lack of support from his colleagues, Gibbon experimented independently. In 1935, he succeeded in keeping a cat alive for twenty-six minutes with a prototype heart-lung machine. After World War II (1939–1945), he continued working on his invention with financial support from the IBM Corportation and produced a machine that worked well with dogs. The first human patient was Cecelia Bavolek who, in 1953, underwent successful open-heart bypass surgery, with Gibbon's heart-lung machine treating her blood. His design was refined at the Mayo clinic in Rochester, Minnesota. A commercial version, the Mayo-Gibbon heart-lung machine, was produced in 1955.

Heart-lung machines

Surgeons cannot operate on a beating heart—it must be stopped. A heart-lung machine, which bypasses the blood flow through the heart and lungs, oxygenates the blood and pumps it through the rest of the patient's body to keep him or her alive while the heart surgery is performed.

When the patient is connected to the heart-lung machine, the heart is stopped using medications or by cooling it. Up to 1.3 gallons (5 liters) of blood are removed from the body, treated, and recirculated each minute.

A patient can be connected to the machine for several hours, but cannot remain connected indefinitely. Eventually, the process of flowing through the heart-lung machine damages the blood, so the time spent on such a machine is limited.

CHAPTER 5

Treating Disease

Modern technology offers many possibilities for making the treatment of disease easier and more comfortable for the patient. Treatments range from minor surgical procedures to life-saving operations and the implantation of devices in the body to keep it working properly.

Helping the heart

Heart disease, which often involves the vessels of the heart as well as the heart muscle itself, is one of the main causes of death in the developed world. Machines and devices can help the heart work, keeping it beating regularly or replacing parts that are damaged.

An artificial pacemaker is a small device implanted in the chest to regulate the heartbeat. It takes over the role of pacemaking cells, a group of cells in the heart, which usually perform this task. If the

CUTTING EDGE SCIENCE

Pacemaker statistics

- Heart failure affects about five million Americans.
- Heart failure costs the United States about $40 billion a year and accounts for 5 to 10 percent of hospital admissions and 6.5 million hospital days annually.
- Between 1990 and 2002, 2.25 million pacemakers were fitted to patients in the United States.
- More than seventeen thousand pacemakers were removed in that same time period because of defects—half because of battery or capacitor failure. The failure rate for pacemakers is 0.68 percent.
- Sixty-six patients died because of malfunctioning pacemakers.

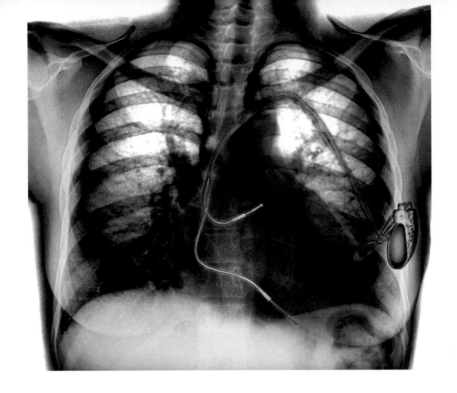

An X-ray reveals the pacemaker (blue) in a patient's body. The pacemaker is not implanted inside the chest cavity. It is implanted just under the skin.

natural pacemaking cells are destroyed or damaged by disease, or stop working because of age, they may produce an irregular heartbeat. An artificial pacemaker can replace the cells' function and keep the patient alive for many years. Wires from the artificial pacemaker carry electrical impulses to the heart muscles to make them contract, causing the heart to beat. Pacemakers use lithium batteries that normally last about seven years and are then replaced in a minor operation.

Early pacemakers were cumbersome external machines, connected to the patient with wires. The first pacemaker to be implanted in a human patient was designed in 1958 by Rune Elmqvist of Sweden. Early models weighed around 6.5 ounces (180 grams). Today, pacemakers weigh only about 1 ounce (30 grams).

The earliest pacemakers controlled the heart all the time, taking over from the heart's own pacemaking cells completely. Demand pacemakers have been in use since the mid-1960s. These take over only when necessary—when the heart is beating too slowly or too quickly. Since the 1970s, programmable pacemakers have been available. Their settings can be adjusted by radio control without surgery. Pacemakers developed in the mid-1980s respond to a body's need for an increased or decreased heart rate. More recent models "learn" a patient's own pattern of heart activity under different conditions and adjust to mimic it. A record of the patient's condition over time can also be downloaded for checkups.

An artificial heart valve is ready to be pulled into place and secured inside the heart.

A new Biotronik pacemaker, developed in 2004, communicates by wireless network with a health care provider, sending information on a patient's condition. Patients don't need to attend a clinic for checkups and can live a more normal life—and medical staff are alerted immediately if there are any problems. Soon, transplanted pacemaker cells may be able to restore the natural pacemaking function of the heart without mechanical aids.

Replacement valves

Some heart problems are caused by faulty valves in the heart. The valves ensure that blood flows through the heart in the right direction. A valve is like a one-way gate that is kept open by the flow of blood in one direction. Blood pushing on it from the other

CUTTING EDGE   MOMENTS

Heart valve history

1952	Charles Hufnagel (U.S.) develops the first mechanical valve for the heart. Used in the aorta, it is a ball valve that moves up and down in a metal cage with the pressure of blood behind it.
1960	Albert Starr (U.S.) performs the first successful replacement of the mitral valve (the valve between the left ventricle and left atrium), using a design developed with engineer Lowell Edwards. The Starr-Edwards valve was made from a steel cage enclosing a silicone rubber ball.
1969	The Bjork-Shiley tilting disk valve is introduced in the U.S. after a high mortality rate (high death rate) is recorded among patients with a narrow aorta who received ball valves.
1979	The first bileaflet valve, the St. Jude Medical valve, is developed in the U.S. It has two semicircular flaps called leaflets that rotate around struts, and it mimics a natural valve more closely than a tilting disk or ball valve.

direction closes it. Faulty, weakened, or damaged valves can be replaced by artificial valves.

Two types of mechanical heart valve can be sewn into the heart during open-heart surgery. One operates like a door, much like the original valve, opening in the correct direction when the pressure is great enough. The other, a ball valve, seals shut with pressure to stop blood from flowing the wrong way. The mechanical valves work indefinitely and never need replacing, but patients need to take blood-thinning drugs for the rest of their lives to avoid the danger of blood clots blocking the valve.

Biological heart valves are also of two types: either removed intact from the heart of another animal (usually a pig) or put on a metal frame from heart valve tissue from a horse or cow. Complete valves from another animal can lead to rejection problems when the recipient's immune system recognizes the valve as "foreign." Antirejection drugs help combat this response. Rejection is not a problem with the second type of valve mentioned here. Patients do not need blood-thinning drugs with biological valves, but they may wear out after about fifteen years and need replacing.

Scientists hope to make future improvements to existing valves by growing tissue over a matrix (a structural framework) to make a biological replacement valve. The best tissue to use would be from the patient's own heart to avoid rejection reactions.

Artificial hearts

Sometimes, serious heart disease or damage caused by blood vessel blockages makes the heart unable to function properly. An artificial heart may be used to take over the function of the heart. The artificial hearts currently available serve only as temporary remedy while a patient waits for a healthy donor heart to become available for a transplant.

An artificial heart replaces the two ventricles—the lower chambers of the heart—with two mechanical pumps. These pump blood into the upper two chambers of the heart, called the atria (which are left in place). The artificial heart is usually made of plastic, aluminum, and polyester.

It is powered by an external battery. A system of compressed air hoses enters the heart through the chest to operate the pumping mechanism. These hoses pose a risk of infection. The equipment is cumbersome. Artificial hearts are not a long-term solution to heart disease.

Of the two lower chambers of the heart, the left ventricle is the more powerful pump because it pumps blood to the entire body.

CUTTING EDGE   MOMENTS

Artificial hearts

In 1957, Willem Kolff, a Dutch-born scientist working in the United States, tested an artificial heart in animals to identify problems. In 1969, a team led by Denton Cooley at St. Luke's Episcopal Hospital, Houston, Texas, successfully implanted an artificial heart in a patient who survived more than sixty hours. One of the best-known artificial hearts, the Jarvik-7, was developed during the late 1970s by U.S. surgeon Robert Jarvik. The Jarvik-7 was successfully used in patients beginning in the early 1980s. In 1982, a patient lived for 112 days with a Jarvik-7 heart. In 1985, a Jarvik-7 kept a patient alive for one week before he had a heart transplant.

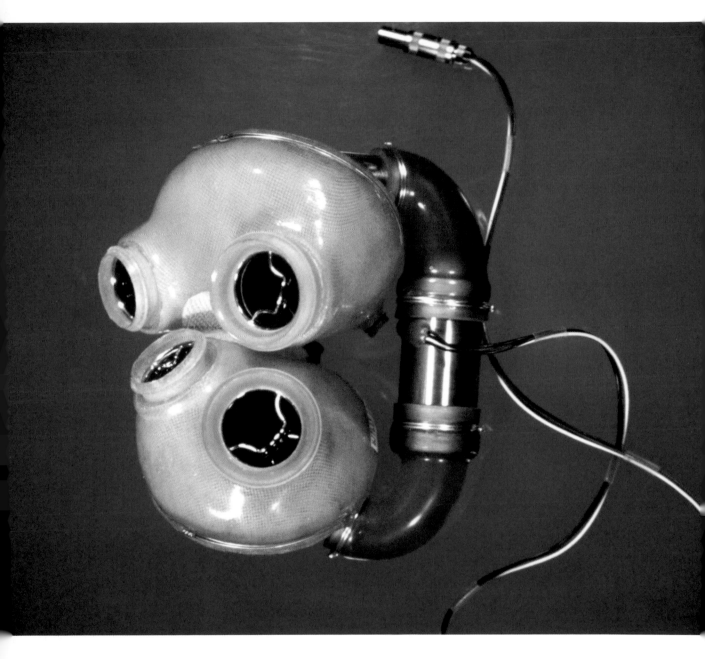

When the heart is diseased, the left ventricle is often not strong enough to work properly, and the patient needs a new heart. While the patient waits for a healthy donor heart to become available for transplant, he or she may have a machine implanted in the heart to help the left ventricle. This device is called a left ventricle assist device (LVAD). An LVAD boosts the functioning of the left ventricle; it does not take over from it completely.

A Jarvik-7 artificial heart is made of aluminum and plastic. The Jarvik-7 was used in the first implant operation in 1982.

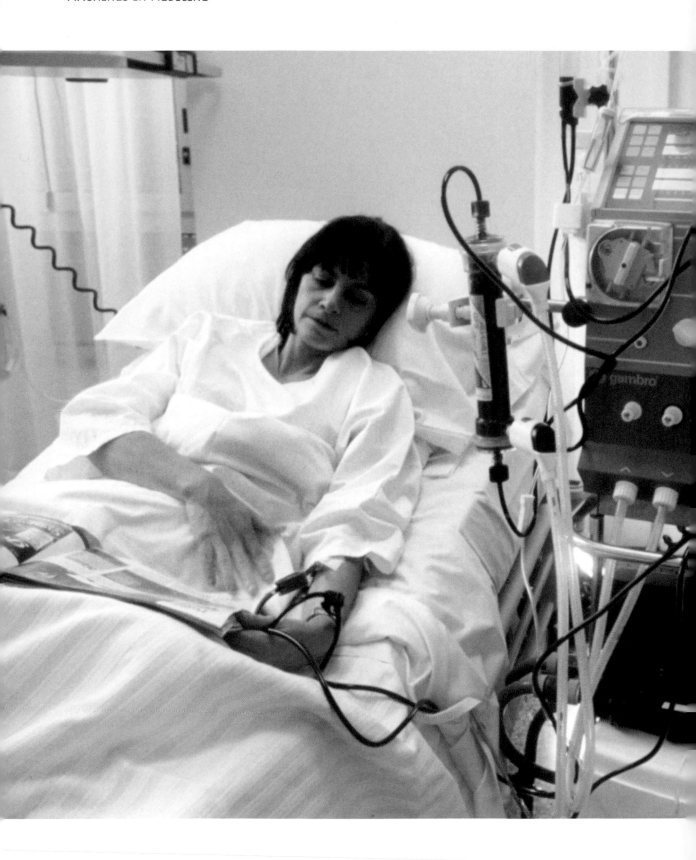

An LVAD draws blood from the left ventricle through a tube to a pump that sends it into the aorta. The pump is implanted in the upper part of the patient's abdomen. It connects through the wall of the abdomen to an external battery and control system. LVADs are small enough to carry around, so a patient has an acceptable standard of living while waiting for a heart transplant.

The latest models of LVADs can be used over an extended period, even replacing heart surgery as a method of treatment. They can be used when a transplanted heart is rejected. An LVAD also gives a weakened heart time to strengthen itself and regain its function. Some doctors consider an LVAD a "bridge to transplant," and use the device as a temporary measure until a donor organ is available.

Some LVADs intended for permanent use have the pump as well as the battery outside the body. They are connected to the heart by a tube that enters the body at the groin.

Kidney problems

The kidneys maintain the water balance of the body by removing waste products through urine. Failure of the kidneys (renal failure) due to damage or disease can be fatal. Machines can take over the function of the kidneys until they recover or until a kidney for transplant is located. In a process called dialysis, an artificial kidney machine (also known as a dialysis machine, or dialyzer) removes waste from the blood outside the patient's body before returning the cleaned blood to the body through a vein in the patient's arm.

CUTTING EDGE   SCIENCE

Kidney dialysis

A tube carries blood from an artery in the patient's forearm into a dialysis machine, where it passes over a thin, "one-way" membrane, or sheet of porous material. A reservoir of a sterile solution is on the other side of the membrane. Impurities in the blood can pass through the membrane, but blood cells are too large to pass through. Before re-entering the body through a vein in the forearm, the blood passes through a trap that remove clots and bubbles. The membranes used in dialysis machines were originally made from animal tissue, but now a layer of hollow cellophane fibers is used.

Opposite: A patient undergoing kidney dialysis.

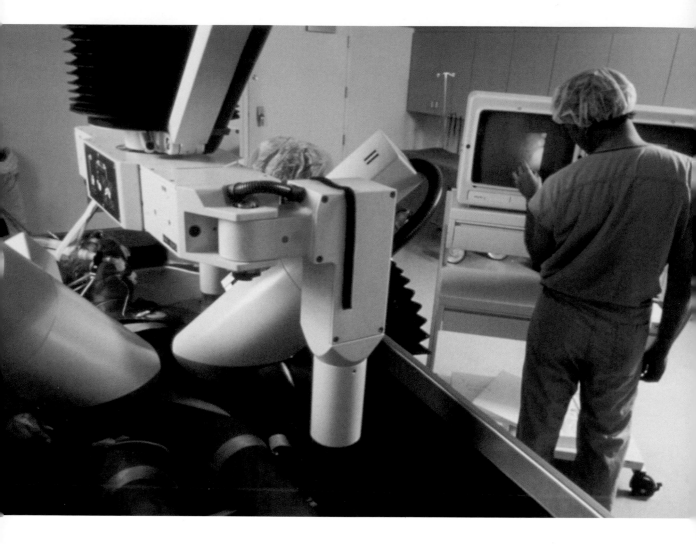

A dialysis patient must be connected to the dialysis machine, either at a hospital or (sometimes) at home, several times a week for about three hours at a time. About one hundred million dialysis treatments take place each year around the world.

Kidney dialysis was first tried on animals in 1913 and on a human patient in 1924. The first practical dialyzer was produced by Dutchmen Willem Kolff and Henrick Berk in 1943. They used a drum with 100 to 130 feet (30 to 40 meters) of cellophane tubing wrapped around it, which rotated in a 26.5-gallon (100-liter) tank of dialyzing solution.

Although the principle worked, the need to puncture an artery and vein each time limited the number of dialysis treatments that each patient could endure. Dialysis became a long-term solution

During lithotripsy treatment to break up kidney stones, the patient may be submerged in a tub of water. The water helps transmit the sound waves.

only with the invention of the shunt in 1960 by U.S. scientists Belding Scribner and Wayne Quinton. This was a U-shaped tube made of nonstick Teflon that was permanently connected to an artery and vein in the patient's arm. The dialyzer could be plugged into the shunt repeatedly without damaging the blood vessels. The shunt was left in place between treatments. This type of shunt is still used today, but it is made from a different material.

Smashing stones

Sometimes, chemicals form hard lumps called stones in the kidney, bladder, or gall bladder. These can be very painful and must be removed. As an alternative to surgery, such stones can be blasted apart using ultrasound or an electrical current. This process is called lithotripsy.

An alternative to using ultrasound for lithotripsy is using shock waves produced by electricity. A probe is inserted into the bladder, usually through the urinary tract, to the stone. An electric current is delivered through the probe to break up the stone.

Lasers may be used if the stone does not respond to lithotripsy treatment. The laser beam must be delivered directly to the stone to avoid damaging other tissues, so the doctor will insert an endoscope (a thin, flexible tube) into the urinary tract up to the location of the stone in the bladder. If the stone is in the kidney, it is reached through a small incision in the patient's back.

CUTTING EDGE   SCIENCE

Sound treatment

Ultrasound is a very high pitched sound that cannot be heard by the human ear. Like all sound, it is transmitted as vibrations through the air and through solid matter. Ultrasound can be used with a lithotripter to break up stones. A lithotripter is a device that focuses ultrasound waves on the stone with the help of X-ray guidance while the patient sits in a tub of water. The stone breaks up and is passed out of the body in the patient's urine.

Focused ultrasound can also be used to treat some kinds of cancer and Parkinson's disease (a nervous disorder). It can also relieve joint pain by heating up specifically targeted body areas without affecting other parts of the body.

CHAPTER 6

Quality of Life

Not all diseases and tissue damage is curable, even with the huge advances in medical science and technology made over recent decades. When doctors cannot cure a patient, they try to provide for him or her the best quality of life possible. Medications and devices that help the patient live with his or her condition comfortably and independently are also prescribed.

Mechanical joints

As people get older, their joints often deteriorate. The combination of years of use, the gradual loss of elasticity in the body tissues, and

CUTTING EDGE   MOMENTS

New hips for old

The earliest recorded attempt at a hip replacement was in 1891 in Germany, using ivory to replace the top of the femur (thigh bone). Steel or chrome replacement joints became widely used in the 1930s, but truly successful hip replacement began with John Charnley's work at the Manchester Royal Infirmary in Manchester, Enland, in the early 1960s. Charnley developed the combination of a metal bone shaft and ball with a socket lined with plastic. His pioneering technique and design have been used ever since, with only slight refinement and changes of material.

The surgeon cuts away the bone of the socket in the hip and the ball shape at the top of the thigh bone and replaces these with metal substitutes. The cup of the socket is lined with polyethylene (a plastic) so that the joint moves smoothly, without friction. The joint may be cemented in place, or its position may be fixed through natural bone growth; that is, new bone will grow to fill the gaps left by surgery.

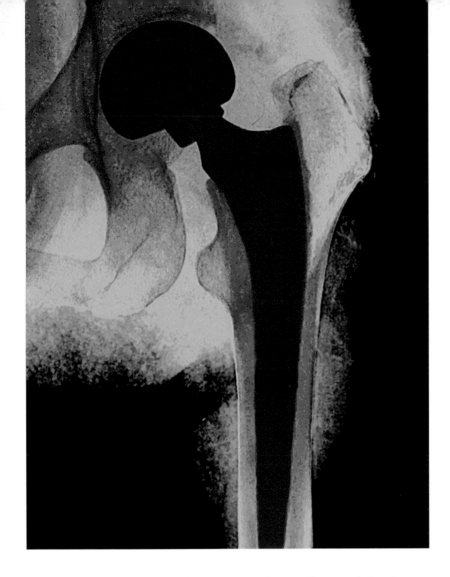

An X-ray of an artificial hip that has replaced a diseased or damaged hip joint. The metal of the implant extends into the femur (thighbone).

the buildup of mineral deposits at the surfaces of the bones contribute to conditions that make joints stiff and painful. Osteoarthritis, a disease in which bone and cartilage wear away, is particularly common in older people. Artificial versions of many joints, including hip, shoulder, elbow, knee, and knuckle, are now available for replacing those that have worn out.

Replacement joints copy the shape and mechanics of the original. Materials for joints must be strong, durable, resistant to wear and tear, and stable when inside the body. Early models made of stainless steel corroded to some degree. Modern replacement joints are made from alloys (mixtures) of other metals, including molybdenum and titanium used with polyethylene. Recently, some surgeons have performed bone resurfacing of the problem joint instead of replacement. They remove the surface of the joint and use a polyethylene coating to restore smooth movement.

New limbs

If a patient loses a limb through an accident or disease, or is born with a limb missing, a prosthetic (replacement) limb can often give him or her much of the capability of a real limb.

People have been using primitive artificial limbs for thousands of years. The earliest were simple wooden props to replace missing legs or hooks to restore the most basic use of a hand. Modern artificial limbs look highly realistic, being made of plastics that are carefully matched to the patient's skin color and limb shape. They also reproduce much of the functionality of the original limb. The latest prosthetic limbs contain electronic sensors that detect nerve impulses in the muscle to which they are attached. Microprocessors process the signals that control the limb, so the person can move the prosthesis in the same way as he or she would move a natural limb.

Artificial limbs are becoming increasingly realistic and sophisticated. The Dextra artificial hand has computer-driven mechanical fingers connected to the user's existing nerve pathways. The hand can be controlled just like real fingers. Pressure sensors in the fingertips allow the user to adjust his or her grip to hold even delicate objects. Scientists are also developing artificial limbs that can be controlled by thought. Sensors in the limbs detect impulses directly from the brain.

CUTTING EDGE   SCIENCE

Cochlear implants

People who are completely deaf may have a cochlear implant—a small device fitted behind the ear and partly inside the head. It provides a way of understanding sound that is not quite the same as hearing: A noise "heard" with an implant may not sound the same as one heard in the normal sense. A cochlear implant picks up and processes sound, concentrating on the sounds relating to speech, and then converts the sounds to an electric current. The current is passed directly to the auditory nerve, so that the cochlear implant bypasses the non-functioning ear. The sound processing usually works on the patterns of speech, so that the wearer can understand speech. Often, it works well enough that the person can understand a telephone conversation as well as face-to-face communication.

A robotic prosthetic hand is sensitive enough to hold an egg. The batteries in this prototype last only twelve hours at a time, but the design allows for promising future developments.

Aids to hearing

People who cannot hear well often use a hearing aid to amplify sounds. This sits behind the ear or just inside it, in the outer ear. The hearing aid picks up sounds, which are transmitted as vibrations in the air, and converts them into an electric current. The current is then amplified and converted back into a sound at a louder intensity than the original. A traditional hearing aid can only help someone who has some level of hearing, since it works by magnifying sounds.

The newer digital hearing aids are more adaptable than traditional models. They can be set to suit each person's hearing loss and needs, and can be adjusted to work well in different environments, such as a football stadium or a quiet library.

Increasingly sensitive cochlear implants (*see sidebar on page 50*) should soon enable deaf people to enjoy music. The new style of implant has four elements that vibrate in response to sound. Each responds at a different range of frequencies. As it vibrates, the implant produces a tiny electrical current that passes to the auditory nerve (the nerve that carries sound information to the brain). The

This retinal implant responds to light and passes an electrical impulse to the optic nerve. It simulates vision for blind patients.

implant's elements are coated with a special material that produces a small voltage without needing a separate battery or power supply. The new design may be available for use in about 2015.

New sight

While people with vision impairment can often use eyeglasses or contact lenses to improve their sight, people with complete or partial vision loss may soon be able to use special glasses that send visual information to a 0.12-inch (3 mm) -long computerized implant inside the eye.

Taking medicinal drugs

Some patients, such as diabetics (people with diabetes), need to take drugs for an extended period of time or even for their entire lives to regulate their disease. Diabetes is a condition in which the patient's body does not produce insulin (the chemical that regulates the blood sugar levels). Type I diabetics (those born with the disease) need to take insulin daily to remain healthy. Type II diabetics may be able to control their disease by diet and medications other than insulin.

New methods of administering long-term medications can make life more comfortable for patients and can remove or reduce the danger of suffering ill effects from forgetting to take medications.

CUTTING EDGE　　SCIENCE

Bionic eye

Researchers at Stanford University, in Stanford, California, developed special goggles that incorporate a video camera and a computer chip implanted behind the patient's retina. The video camera picks up the image in front of the person's eyes and uses a wireless connection to send it to a computer the size of a wallet. The computer processes the information and sends an image back to the goggles, which reflect the image into the eye. The implant has light-sensitive electric cells that are fired by the image. The chip converts the information to electrical pulses in the same way as cells in the retina. It passes these to cells deep in the retina for transmission to the optical nerve (the nerve that carries information from the eye to the brain). This device gives the user some experience of sight.

Some drugs can be delivered by implanting a slow-release capsule in the body, called an implanted drug delivery system (IDDS). The drug is released at a steady rate over months or even years. For example, the use of contraceptive implants in the arm can protect women against pregnancy for up to five years. The implant is a small, flexible rod that releases hormones at a steady rate. There are different types of IDDS:

Biodegradable and nonbiodegradable implants A biodegradable implant slowly breaks down in the body, releasing the drug built into it. A nonbiodegradable implant does not break down. Both types release drugs passively at a steady rate.

Pumped implant This uses a tiny, remote-controlled pump to adjust the rate of delivery of a drug. It can be useful to deliver pain relief for example, by enabling adjustment of the amount of drugs to suit the patient's needs.

Radiation therapy implants Radiation therapy is a type of cancer treatment that uses radiation to destroy cancerous cells. Radiation

CUTTING EDGE   DEBATES

Who chooses whether to implant?

Some of the best drugs for treating psychotic disorders, such as schizophrenia, can be delivered by IDDS. This avoids the difficulty of disturbed or distressed patients forgetting to take medication, and releases them and their carers from the burden of remembering to take daily medications. The issue raises ethical concerns about the rights of patients, however. Some psychiatric patients are not able to make an informed choice about implants. Ethicists debate whether it is right to use implants in patients who refuse to take medicines but could become dangerous to themselves or others without medication.

Patients' rights groups argue that implanting devices to release mind-altering drugs gives medical staff unacceptable levels of control over patients and could be used more for the convenience of the medical staff than for the patients. Without a long track record to establish the safety of the system, vulnerable patients may be exposed to risks to which they are incapable of consenting.

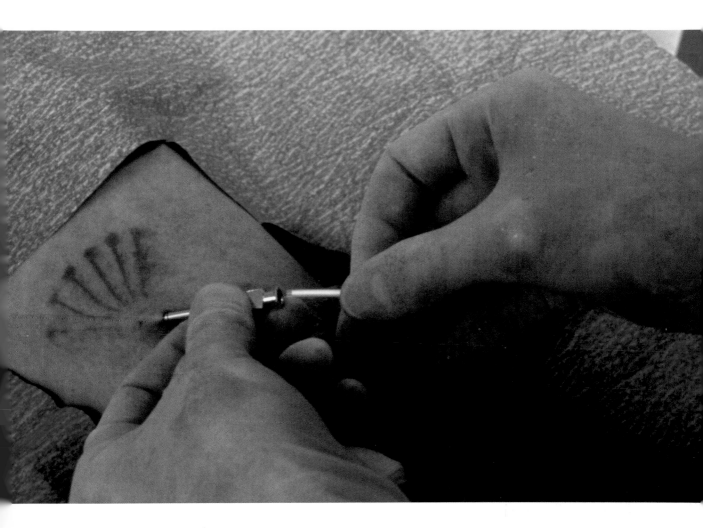

therapy implants can help cancer patients by providing ongoing, targeted medication in the area in which cancerous cells are growing. By treating only the affected area, the unpleasant and damaging side effects caused by exposing large areas of the body to radiation therapy are minimized.

Plastic-coated implants A plastic coating on implants in the heart and vessels often contains drugs that are released steadily. New "smart" plastic films may soon be able to release different drugs in sequence over a set time period. Plastic coatings form barrier layers that are slowly broken down in the body; drugs are sandwiched between the plastic layers. The coatings would be used on implants, such as replacement joints, to deliver the drugs needed and optimize the body's acceptance and use of the joint.

A doctor inserts a contraceptive implant under the skin of a woman's arm. Ink marks on the skin indicate the sites of the implants. The slow release of a hormone will provide contraception for five years.

CHAPTER 7

In the Future

The future of medicine will see an increased use of computer technology, especially of nanotechnology and miniaturized systems that can be implanted in the body. Wireless connections allow remote control of computers inside the body and the transmission of information from inside to external computers and monitors. Miniaturization will advance, too, with nanotechnology (microscopic machinery) opening up entirely new avenues of diagnosis and treatment.

Hopes for the heart

Implantable "smart chips" that monitor the heart, assess its beating rate and pattern, and give early warning of heart attacks, are already emerging. A new implant the size of a grain of rice is being developed to measure pressure inside the cardiac chambers.

This boy can play a computer game by using a sensor attached to his finger to relay brain impulses to the computer.

The implant has no batteries and is powered by a radio transmitter and receiver waved over it. When triggered by a signal from the transmitter, the implant sends its stored information to the receiver. An implantable chip could help people who suffer from fluid build-up in the heart. They could avoid an unpleasant surgical procedure now required several times a year to check on the condition of their heart.

Thought control

In 2000, neurobiologist Miguel Nicolelis at Duke University in Durham, North Carolina, trained a monkey to move a robotic arm by thought using nerve impulses picked up by electrodes implanted in its brain. Researchers at the Institut Dalle Molle d'Intelligence Artificielle Perceptive (Dalle Molle Institute for Perceptual Artificial Intelligence, or IDIAP) in Martigny, Switzerland, are now developing a robotic system that will allow people to control wheelchairs or prosthetic limbs just by thinking. The system uses electrical impulses from the brain to relay "thoughts" to computer technology that controls the devices.

CUTTING EDGE — SCIENCE

Harnessing brainwaves

The brain cells that control limbs remain active even if the limbs are severed. This continuing ability could be harnessed to move an artificial limb or some other device. Wireless electrodes implanted in the brain, or in a removable cap of electrodes, would communicate with the technologies the person wanted to control. A computer would analyze the signals picked up from the brain by the electrodes and look for the unique patterns of activity associated with different types of movement. Another wireless connection would send instructions for movement to a controlled device, such as a robotic limb or wheelchair.

Nanotechnology

Nanotechnology is the science of making very small machinery that can work in tiny spaces, even inside the human body. Nanotechnology works with tiny computer components so small that they are measured in nanometers (millionths of a millimeter), smaller than a single cell.

The goal of many nanotechnology pioneers is to produce devices that work independently. In medical applications, that may mean that these devices will independently navigate the inside of the body. Nanotechnology is in its infancy, but its potential applications in medicine are great. Through nanotechnology, it may be possible one day to send microscopic machines into the body to perform repairs and monitor a person's health.

Computer art image
of nanorobots working
on brain cells.

A team of researchers at the Chinese Academy of Sciences in Beijing, China, is already developing tiny robots that could be put into blood vessels and "swim" around—breaking up any blood clots they encounter. These robots would be propelled by a magnetic field applied from outside the body. At 0.12 inch (3 mm), the robots are far too large to count as nanotechnology. As the technology develops, however, medical researchers hope to build microscopic devices that will navigate their way through the body, fixing problems and constantly monitoring the body's health. These devices could, for example, destroy cancer cells and other harmful structures, or even work inside cells to correct the DNA in faulty genes responsible for inherited disorders. Nano-tools could help organize or promote the growth and reproduction of cells to encourage healing or regenerate organs, clean up the blood vessels or lungs, and control prosthetic devices.

Computers everywhere

Computers are already widely used in hospitals and clinics. Increasingly, implants and prostheses used by patients will communicate wirelessly with computers to allow instant access to a patient's condition. Machinery used inside the patient's body will become more responsive, monitoring and adjusting to changing conditions and needs.

In addition, computers will play a greater role in the training of medical staff. Several organizations are producing virtual reality systems that allow doctors to experience some of the symptoms their patients endure, including systems that simulate heart disease, several types of blindness, schizophrenia, and stroke. The training aids help medical staff empathize with patients and better understand their needs and limitations. More virtual reality systems will likely emerge, both to help doctors understand medical conditions and to train them safely in surgical procedures.

CUTTING EDGE MOMENTS

Nanotubules kill cancer cells

In 2005, researchers at Stanford University in California discovered that they could destroy cancer cells and leave normal cells unharmed using a combination of nanotubules (nano-scale tubes of carbon), and a laser. The nanotubules are only half the width of a DNA molecule, and thousands can fit into a single cell.

Some cancer cells have receptors on their surface for a vitamin called folate, but normal cells do not. Researchers exploited (used) this difference to ensure that only cancerous cells absorbed the nanotubules. In the body, a laser directed at the area of the cancer would then rapidly heat the nanotubules of carbon, exploding the cells. Normal cells are unaffected by the laser. Tests on tissue in the laboratory show that the system works, but human trials have not yet begun.

Glossary

anemia A condition in which a person has too few red blood cells in his or her blood.

anesthetic A drug which causes a person to lose sensation and feel no pain. A general anesthetic puts a person to "sleep" for surgery, and a local anesthetic numbs only part of the body.

aorta The large blood vessel that carries blood from the left ventricle of the heart to the rest of the body.

artery A thick-walled blood vessel that carries blood from the heart to the body or lungs.

atria (plural of atrium) The two upper chambers of the heart.

bacteria (plural of bacterium) Microorganisms present in soil, air, and water that can cause disease.

cancerous growth An abnormal growth or tumor caused by cancerous cells. Cancer is a disease in which a group or groups of cells begin to grow uncontrollably.

cardiologist A doctor who specializes in treating the heart and related blood circulation problems.

carpal tunnel syndrome A condition in which a nerve in the wrist is compressed, which can compromise the use of the hand or cause painful or uncomfortable sensations.

chromosome One of twenty-three long structures that form inside the cell nucleus of humans during cell division. Chromosomes carry the genes (DNA).

cornea The transparent layer covering the front of the eyeball.

deoxyribonucleic acid (DNA) A complex protein from which chromosomes are built that holds the code for the genetic makeup of an organism.

diabetes A condition in which the body cannot produce insulin (the hormone that controls blood sugar levels) or does not respond properly to it, causing excess sugar in the blood.

diagnosis A study of symptoms to figure out what is wrong with a patient.

dialysis The process of cleansing the blood of impurities artificially.

dialyzer A machine used for dialysis.

embryo An early stage of development of an unborn baby, from a few days to eight weeks after fertilization.

enzyme A natural protein that speeds up the chemical reactions that are essential to life.

epidemic A rapid, widespread outbreak of an infectious disease.

epilepsy A disorder of the nervous system causing periodic loss of consciousness.

forceps A medical tool similar to tongs, used for holding or pulling.

gene A section of a chromosome that contains the genetic coding for a single characteristic.

heart attack A serious condition in which the heart muscle receives an insufficient blood supply, usually because of interrupted blood flow.

heart-lung machine A machine that replaces the function of the heart and lungs during an operation; it oxygenates and pumps the blood.

immune system The body's defense against disease and invading organisms. The immune system fights and destroys cells it does not recognize as "self."

incubator A special crib used for newborn babies in which temperature and atmosphere are controlled.

insulin A hormone produced by the pancreas that controls the level of sugar in the blood.

laser A powerful, precisely focused beam of light.

leukemia Cancer of the blood cells.

matrix A part of tissue that is not composed of cells but provides the structural framework.

membrane A very fine layer of tissue.

muscular dystrophy A group of disorders causing progressive muscle weakness and wasting.

nanotechnology Technology that uses components on a microscopic scale, measured in nanometers (a millionth of a millimeter).

nanotubules Very tiny cylinders a few nanometers in diameter (a nanometer is a millionth of a millimeter).

neonatal Relating to newborn babies.

nerves Bundles of cells that carry messages to, from, and within the brain as electrical impulses.

nervous system The system of nerves, spine cord, and brain that processes information coming into the body and gives out instructions to control and move the body, including involuntary actions such as digestion, breathing, and temperature regulation.

neurobiologist A person who specializes in the study of how nervous systems work in humans or other animals.

nuclei (plural of nucleus) The control center of a cell; also contains the genetic material.

osteoarthritis A disease caused by the breakdown of cartilage in the joints, resulting in stiffness and pain.

pacemaker A device implanted under the skin to transmit electrical pulses through a wire inserted in the heart to regulate the heartbeat.

polio A serious infection that invades the nervous system and affects muscle control, which can cause permanent paralysis.

prosthetic Relating to an artificial replacement for a body part.

protein A substance that makes up living structures, such as muscle, and controls processes inside cells.

psychiatric Relating to mental illness.

psychotic Relating to mental illness that makes people believe things that are not real.

rejection The body's immune system reaction to expel or kill implanted tissues or organs that it considers "foreign," or "not self."

respirometer A device designed to measure the rate of respiration (breathing).

retina The inside surface of the back of the eye that contains the cells that process light and colors.

schizophrenia A serious mental illness in which a person cannot distinguish between actual and imaginary expeiences.

sepsis A bacterial infection of the blood.

side effects Unwanted effects of a drug or other treatment.

smear test ("pap test") The removal of a few cells from the cervix (neck of the uterus) for cancer testing.

stroke A change in blood supply to the brain; often causes temporary or permanent loss of movement, speech, or another ability.

symptom An abnormal sensation or change in bodily function experienced by a patient.

transplant The replacement of a diseased or damaged organ with a healthy organ from another person or animal.

ultrasound Waves of very high frequency sound.

ventilator A machine that assists breathing.

ventricle One of the two lower chambers of the heart.

vital signs Biological signs that show a person's state of health. They include breathing, heartbeat, blood pressure, and body temperature.

Further Information

BOOKS

Kevles, Bettyann Holzmann. *Naked to the Bone: Medical Imaging in the Twentieth Century.* Perseus (1998).

Kjelle, Marylou Morano. *Raymond Damadian and the Development of MRI.* Unlocking the Secrets of Science (Series). Mitchell Lane (2002).

McClafferty, Carla Killough. *The Head Bone's Connected To The Neck Bone: The Weird, Wacky, and Wonderful X-Ray.* Farrar, Straus and Giroux (BYR) (2001).

Rooney, Anne. *Medicine.* The Cutting Edge (series). Heinemann Library (2005).

Rooney, Anne. *Medicine Now.* Chrysalis (2003).

Wolbarst, Anthony Brinton. *Looking Within: How X-Ray, CT, MRI, Ultrasound, and Other Medical Image Are Created, and How They Help Physicians Save Lives.* University of California Press (1999).

Townsend, John. *Scalpels, Stitches and Scars: A History of Surgery.* A Painful History of Medicine (series). Raintree (2006).

WEB SITES

www.makingthemodernworld.org.uk/ icons_of_invention/medicine/
Follow the development of medical inventions from 1750 to 2000.

www.medicalnewstoday.com/sections/ medical_devices/
Choose a link to learn about the latest developments and breakthroughs in medical technology.

www.newscientist.com/home.ns
Read about the latest developments in medical technologies and treatments in the weekly journal *New Scientist*.

www.nctn.hq.nasa.gov/innovation/innovation 112/2-coverstory.html
Discover how advances in space technology have changed the course of modern medicine and influenced the development of innovative medical equipment.

Publisher's note to educators and parents: Our editors have carefully reviewed these Web sites to ensure that they are suitable for children. Many Web sites change frequently, however, and we cannot guarantee that a site's future contents will continue to meet our high standards of quality and educational value. Be advised that children should be closely supervised whenever they access the Internet.

Index

Index *(continued)*